DIKEMBE MUTOMBO

MOUNT MUTOMBO

By Philip Brooks

CHILDRENS PRESS ®

CHICAGO

Photo Credits

Cover, Tim DeFrisco/AllSport USA; 5, ©Tim DeFrisco; 6, Tim DeFrisco/AllSport USA; 9 (top), Grolier, Inc., The New Book of Knowledge; 9 (right), ©Tim DeFrisco; 10, ©David L. Johnson/Sports Photo Masters, Inc.; 13, Reuters/Bettmann; 15, AP/Wide World; 16, Courtesy Georgetown University Sports Information; 19, Reuters/Bettmann; 21, Courtesy Georgetown University Sports Information; 22 (left), ©David L. Johnson/Sports Photo Masters, Inc.; 22 (right), ©Noren Trotman/Sports Photo Masters, Inc.; 25, Reuters/Bettmann; 26, AP/Wide World; 26 (inset), ©Tim DeFrisco; 29, Focus on Sports; 31 (top), Courtesy Georgetown University Sports Information; 31(bottom), ©Tim DeFrisco; 32, ©Noren Trotman/Sports Photo Masters, Inc.; 35, ©David L. Johnson/Sports Photo Masters, Inc.; 36, ©Tim DeFrisco; 39, ©Brian Drake/Sportschrome East/West; 40, 43, ©Tim DeFrisco; 44 (left), Reuters/Bettmann; 44 (right), ©Tim DeFrisco; 45 (left), ©Noren Trotman/Sports Photo Masters, Inc.; 45 (right), ©Tim DeFrisco; 46, Tim DeFrisco/AllSport USA; 47, ©Tim DeFrisco

Editorial Staff

Project Editor: Mark Friedman
Design: Herman Adler Design Group
Photo Editor: Jan Izzo
Intern: Amy Vivio

Library of Congress Cataloging-in-Publication Data

Brooks, Philip. 1963–
      Dikembe Mutombo (Mount Mutombo) / by Philip Brooks.
          p. cm. – (Sports stars)
      Summary: A career biography of the Zairian basketball phenomenon, educated at Georgetown and a star player for the Denver Nuggets.
      Added title page title: Dikembe Mutombo.
      ISBN 0-516-04392-7
      1. Mutombo, Dikembe—Juvenile literature. 2. Basketball players—Zaire—Biography—Juvenile literature. [1. Mutombo, Dikembe.
2. Basketball players. 3. Blacks—Zaire—Biography.] I. Title. II. Series.
GV884.M87B76   1995
796.323'092–dc20   94-14018
[B]   CIP
                                                                          AC

DIKEMBE MUTOMBO
MOUNT MUTOMBO

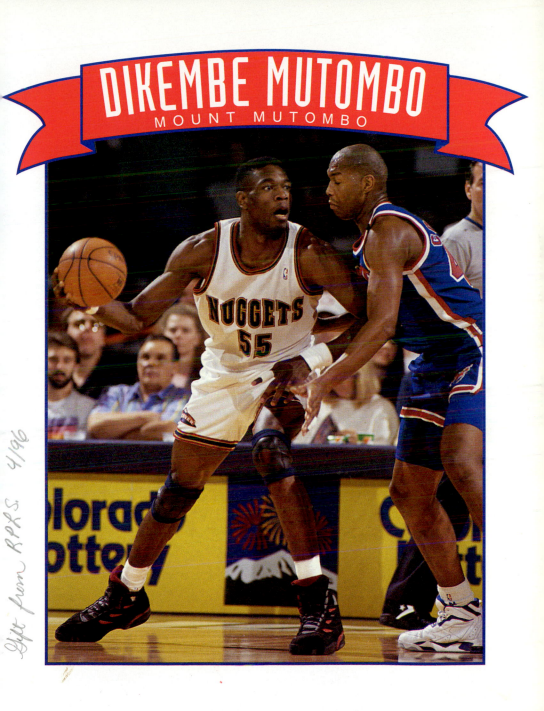

His full name is Dikembe Mutombo Mpolondo Mukamba Diken's Jean Jacque Wa Mutombo. But Dikembe Mutombo's American friends just call him "Deke."

Dikembe is always friendly, polite, and kind. He has a deep voice, and everyone loves to hear his booming laugh. Because he is so happy and outgoing, Dikembe has a lot of American friends. Still, the United States will never feel like home to him. "I have an African soul," he says.

Dikembe grew up in a big city called Kinshasa, in the nation of Zaire. Zaire is in central Africa. Forty million people live there.

As a young man in Kinshasa, Dikembe was always very tall for his age. Sometimes it was difficult to be such a tall person. "I didn't want to go to the market after awhile," he says. "People would run away. 'He is here!' They thought I was a ghost from another planet! Not a kid from the neighborhood. It would make me sad."

★ ★ ★

Sometimes his height even got him into trouble. Teachers thought he was being disrespectful. They believed this because he was always looking down at the tops of their heads. In Africa, this is a sign of disrespect. But Dikembe could not help it.

In 1987, Dikembe left Zaire to come to the United States. He attended Georgetown University in Washington, D.C., on a basketball scholarship. He was 21 years old. In Zaire, he had not played much basketball. He had only read about the National Basketball Association (NBA) in newspapers, and he was 17 years old the first time he ever touched a basketball. He came to Georgetown to play basketball and earn a college degree. Then he planned to go to medical school and become a doctor.

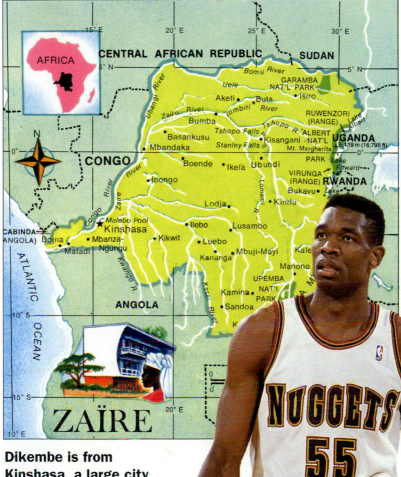

ZAÏRE

Dikembe is from Kinshasa, a large city in western Zaire. He says that even though he plays basketball in the United States, he has an African soul.

Dikembe doing what he does best: blocking a shot. He is perhaps the best shot blocker in the NBA.

It did not work out that way. At Georgetown, Dikembe developed into a great player. Today, he patrols the lane for the Denver Nuggets, and he is recognized as one of the most awesome defensive players in the NBA. At a height of 7-foot-2, he towers over just about every other player. When Dikembe spreads his arms, they span 7 feet, 6 inches. He is also quick on his feet, and he can leap better than just about any center in basketball. He weighs 250 pounds and has almost no fat on his body.

During the 1993-94 NBA season, Dikembe blocked 336 shots. That is an average of more than four every game—the highest average in the league. After swatting away a shot, Dikembe likes to wag his long index finger at the shooter. It's as if he's saying, "No, no, little man!" Nobody looks forward to the task of shooting the ball over "Mount Mutombo."

Dikembe Mutombo is an amazing basketball player. But he is an amazing person, too. He credits his success and happiness to his parents. "I had eight brothers and sisters, and we lived in a large house," he says. "[There were] 17 of us in the house, with cousins and others. My parents made sure...I was raised right. Education was the prime priority for us, and almost everybody in my family has finished college."

Dikembe had a great career at Georgetown University, not only as a ball player, but as a student. First he had to learn to speak English. He worked many hours a day for nearly two years to learn the language. At the same time, he was also learning Spanish and Portuguese! Dikembe came to college already able to speak French, Lingala, Tshiluba, and several other African languages. At Georgetown, he studied diplomacy, which is the way different countries work together and get along without fighting.

Dikembe and Georgetown coach John Thompson

Dikembe also learned a lot about basketball during his four years in college. He has great respect for Georgetown's coach, John Thompson. "The man is not [just] my coach," he says. "When I am around him, I call him 'Daddy.' If not for him, I would not be at this level." Respect for the wisdom of older, more experienced people is a lesson Dikembe learned as a child.

During his junior year in college, Dikembe learned about playing the center position from Bill Russell. Russell was perhaps the greatest defensive center ever. He is in the Basketball Hall of Fame. Dikembe was always willing to listen when Bill Russell talked. After all, Russell had played on 11 championship teams with the Boston Celtics. Dikembe says a ball player would have to be stupid not to listen to Bill Russell. "[Bill] has 11 [championship] rings and only 10 fingers!"

Dikembe believed no one knew more about the game than Bill Russell and Coach Thompson. So he listened to them carefully. He worked hard to improve his game. He knew it was not enough just to be tall and quick. He watched video tapes of Kareem Abdul-Jabbar and Hakeem Olajuwon in order to work on his moves. He learned a hook shot and practiced his dunks.

Dikembe was tutored by Boston Celtics legend Bill Russell. Russell was one of the best centers in NBA history.

While they were Georgetown teammates, Alonzo Mourning (#33) and Dikembe Mutombo (#55) frustrated opposing offenses.

He kept on growing, too. During his freshman year, he wore size 17 shoes. He grew into size 18 in his sophomore season. By his senior year, Dikembe's sneakers were size 20!

At Georgetown, Dikembe played with Alonzo Mourning, whom Dikembe calls "Zo." The 6-foot-10 Mourning now plays for the Charlotte Hornets. At Georgetown, the two were known as the "Twin Towers." Both played center, but they never fought over playing time. They became close friends. In practice, they guarded one another. They played against each other fiercely. This friendly competition in practice helped make both of them stronger players.

Dikembe had to sit out his first season at Georgetown. He was not yet eligible to play under college basketball rules. When he was finally allowed to play, everyone was excited. They wanted to see what he could do on the court. John Thompson had told reporters,

"Y'all are going to love Mutombo." With two great centers, the Georgetown Hoyas would be unbeatable!

Dikembe did not understand all of the pre-season excitement surrounding him. He had not even played a game, so he felt he had not proved himself. "The day I am good, I think all the newspapers will talk about me. But I am not good yet," he said.

But people already liked him. He was popular with reporters and his teammates. For one thing, they loved to hear him speak English. He waved his arms when he spoke. They loved his accent, too. To make sure people understood him, he repeated everything he said several times. Then he would say, "You understand? You understand?" Then he would let out his big, booming laugh. He was just a great guy to be around.

Dikembe's arms together span over seven feet across!

Dikembe played well during the 1988-89 season. But it was not until the Big East Tournament postseason that he showed just how good he could be. In the first game of the tournament, Georgetown faced Boston College. Alonzo Mourning started at center for the Hoyas, but he got into early foul trouble. Dikembe jumped up off the bench. He played very well in his buddy's place. He scored 12 points and blocked two shots in the first half. He went on to play just as well throughout the tournament. In the championship game, Dikembe outplayed Syracuse University's star center, Derrick Coleman. The Hoyas won the game and clinched the Big East championship. Dikembe had proved he was ready for the big time.

That season Dikembe, Alonzo, and the rest of the Hoyas blocked more shots than any team in the nation. Georgetown fans began keeping track of how many blocks the Hoyas made during each game. They brought wooden placards to the games. Each was painted with a big hand. Every time the Hoyas blocked a shot, the fans hung up one

Dikembe jams for Georgetown.

more "hand." Soon enough a line of these
huge hands would form in the stands. Fans
called this "Rejection Row." Visiting teams
dreaded coming to Georgetown.

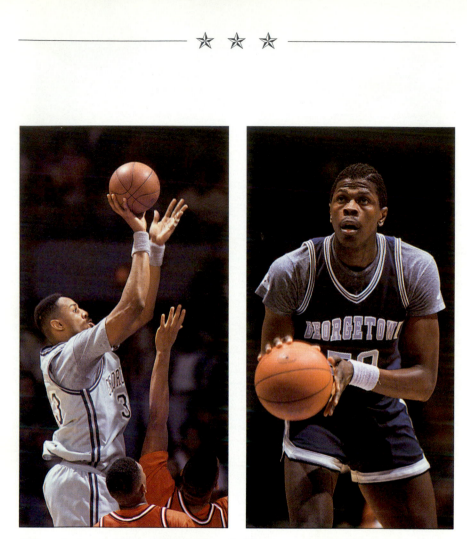

Dikembe and Alonzo Mourning (left) were good friends as Hoya teammates. Now, Dikembe is also close to Patrick Ewing (right), another Georgetown graduate.

A few years earlier, Patrick Ewing had also blocked shots for the Hoyas. Now, he came back to Georgetown as often as he could to watch Dikembe and Alonzo play. He visited practice, too. The three became close friends. They may be the three tallest friends in the world. Together they measure more than 21 feet tall!

During his freshman year at Georgetown, several students came to Dikembe's room one night. "Come outside!" they said. When he came outside, they pointed and smiled. Dikembe saw that it was snowing. His friends thought he had never seen snow before. They imagined that all of Africa was hot and dry. But Zaire is a mountainous country with many snow-covered peaks.

Dikembe's college friends liked to joke with him about Africa. Most of them knew he had grown up in a modern city. Still, they joked that zebras strolled down Dikembe's street, or that Dikembe's neighbors wore bones through their noses and carried spears.

★ ★ ★

Dikembe laughed at his friends' good-natured jokes. But he was sad that none of his American friends had ever seen his homeland. Dikembe longed to show them the Africa he loved so deeply.

Years later, in the summer of 1994, Dikembe got his wish. Alonzo Mourning, Patrick Ewing, and several other NBA players joined him on a goodwill trip to Africa. He said, "It's been almost seven years joking about African tradition and African life. But now it is like a special gift...my friends have given me by coming on this trip."

Dikembe led his friends to South Africa, Somalia, Kenya, and Ethiopia. "Although I am from Zaire," Dikembe says, "I consider all of Africa my home and all Africans my people."

One part of Dikembe's African trip made him unhappy. He could not visit his own family in Zaire. Since 1965, Zaire has been run by a cruel dictator, and through years of unrest, the country has become dangerous. It would be especially dangerous for a rich and famous man like

Mutombo, Ewing, and Mourning tour a South African Village.

Dikembe Mutombo to travel there. So Dikembe has not seen his family since college.

Many of the people Dikembe and his friends saw on their African trip lived in shacks with no running water or electricity. But even these poor people smiled when these NBA stars held special basketball camps for local children. Children who lived miles from the nearest television set pointed and shouted: "You are Dikembe Mutombo from Zaire!" They were proud that an African had become a famous basketball player in the United States.

Dikembe teaches a young girl at one of his basketball camps in South Africa. Dikembe's basketball shoes (inset) are popular around the world—especially in Africa.

Dikembe told everyone he met about his great hopes for Africa. The continent is vast and fertile. "If we can solve our problems, we can be rich," he tells fellow Africans.

Dikembe often travels to Africa, and he works hard for CARE. CARE is a charity that helps to improve life for poor people in Africa. As a child in Zaire, Dikembe learned that people should share their good fortune with their families. If someone becomes rich, that person must help others in need. So Dikembe gets many requests for help from his family and friends. "Every time there is a funeral, I have to pay. If someone needs a place to stay I have to pay. If cousins and nephews need to go to school Mutombo has to pay!" But Dikembe doesn't mind giving money to help others. He realizes how fortunate he is to earn millions of dollars for playing a game he loves.

As late as his junior year at Georgetown, Dikembe was not planning to play in the NBA. He thought he was not good enough to make it in the pros. He was a strong defensive player and rebounder. But he scored only 10.7 points per game. He thought he would never improve enough to compete with his friends Patrick and Alonzo.

That was before Bill Russell gave him some more advice. Bill talked to Dikembe for hours. He convinced Dikembe he could make it in the NBA. Dikembe listened and worked harder than ever. The work paid off, and he had a fine senior year. He raised his scoring average to 15.2 points per game, and he grabbed more than 12 rebounds a game. He was named the Big East Conference's Defensive Player of the Year. He was unanimously voted to the All-Big East team.

★ ★ ★

Dikembe no longer doubted that he would play professional basketball. But that summer, he worked still harder to improve. "I know the NBA is a business," he said. "It's not a place where you can fool around."

At the 1991 NBA draft, the first three teams passed up their chance to draft Dikembe. He watched Larry Johnson go to the Charlotte Hornets. Then Kenny Anderson was chosen by the New Jersey Nets. The Golden State Warriors picked Syracuse's Billy Owens next.

Few were surprised when the Denver Nuggets used the fourth pick to take Dikembe, even though Nuggets head coach Paul Westhead had never seen Dikembe play. The Nuggets desperately needed a center, and they were happy Dikembe was still available. And Westhead was soon very impressed with his new center. "Tell him something once and he'll learn it," Westhead said of Dikembe.

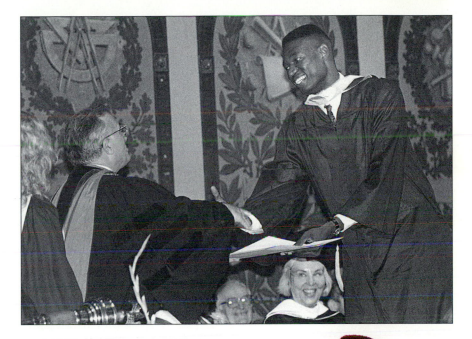

Deke graduates from Georgetown (above) and flashes another smile (below) after being drafted by the Denver Nuggets.

MUTOMBO
55

★ ★ ★

Dikembe's rookie season in the NBA began like a dream. Through the first quarter of the season, he was scoring more than 20 points per game. Every night, Dikembe was outplaying the NBA's best centers. Many people thought he would win the Rookie of the Year award.

He worked even harder because he wanted to be the best center in the game. "I want in every town for people to say 'Mutombo is coming tonight!'" His teammate, backup center Scott Hastings, said, "I've never seen a player work as hard as he does."

The fans voted to make Dikembe the Western Conference's starting center in the 1992 All-Star Game. This is an amazing honor for a rookie. But as the long season wore on, Dikembe grew more and more tired. His knees ached. His muscles weakened. He could not move as quickly as he had at the beginning of the season.

Traveling from city to city wore Dikembe down, too. In March, he injured his thumb and missed the rest of the season. Dikembe's rookie year taught him how hard it is to be an NBA player. Still, he finished second to Charlotte's Larry Johnson in the voting for Rookie of the Year.

Dikembe's rookie season had been exciting. He had great successes and some failures, too. Hurting his thumb must have reminded him of the first time he ever played basketball. That day, he had fallen down on the asphalt court and cut his chin. He still has a scar there. It reminds him of how far he has come, and how much he still has to learn about the game.

Dikembe is still close friends with fellow Georgetown graduates Alonzo Mourning and Patrick Ewing. All three are dominant NBA centers. During the off-season, they meet almost every day to practice in the Georgetown gym. They work hard together. They push each other to get even better. Dikembe learns everything

Now NBA stars, Dikembe and Alonzo are great rivals as well as great friends.

Dikembe goes up for a block against another former Georgetown center, Patrick Ewing.

he can from them. Patrick shows Dikembe how he lowers his shoulder and bumps his defender. This gives him an open shot at the hoop. Alonzo shows Dikembe how he uses his strength to position himself to get a rebound.

Because of his constant extra practice, Dikembe continues to improve his game every year. John Thompson is proud of Dikembe and his other two former Hoyas. He thinks they are great examples for his young players. "Look!" Thompson says. "Patrick, Alonzo, and Dikembe have made it, but they are still back here every summer running wind sprints and playing pickup games like they are trying to make the team!"

Dikembe's happiest moment as a basketball player came during his fourth year in the league. The Nuggets had a mediocre 1993-94 season, finishing with a record of 42-40. They managed to clinch the last playoff spot in their conference. That meant they had to face the team with the best regular-season record, the Seattle

Supersonics. Sportswriters thought Seattle was the best team in basketball. They had won 63 games and lost only 19. Everyone assumed the Nuggets would be just a warm-up for the powerful Sonics and the series would end quickly.

Seattle did win the first two games of the series. If the Nuggets suffered one more loss, they would go home for the summer. To win three straight playoff games after going 0-2 is an almost impossible feat in the NBA playoffs.

But then, the night after their second loss, Dikembe had a dream. In his dream, the Nuggets won three games in a row. He became determined to make his dream come true.

During the next three games, he played better than ever. Dikembe seemed to be everywhere. He challenged every shot and grabbed every rebound in sight. Mount Mutombo swatted away just about every Sonic slam dunk. No shot could get past his long arms and huge hands. No matter how many moves the Sonics threw at Dikembe,

Dikembe fights for a rebound.

he was waiting for them. The inspired Nuggets won the next two games to tie the series.

Still, everyone expected the Sonics to win the deciding game on their home court. They had been such a powerful team during the season. It seemed impossible that the Nuggets could beat them three times in a row.

But the Nuggets fought hard all night long, and with only seconds remaining, they held a slim lead. As the clock ran down, Seattle All-Star Shawn Kemp drove the lane, trying to score and save the Sonics. Swat! Kemp's shot disappeared with a flick of Dikembe Mutombo's wrist.

Dikembe fell to the floor and lay on his back, smiling from ear to ear. He was overwhelmed with joy. The Nuggets had done it! Dikembe's dream had come true.

The Nuggets had not peaked yet. They went on to beat the Utah Jazz in the next round. After blocking 31 shots against Seattle, Dikembe rejected a record 38 Utah shots in the second round. But after knocking off Utah, the Nuggets' dream ride came to an end. The eventual NBA champions, the Houston Rockets, eliminated the Nuggets in the Western Conference Finals.

In 1994-95, Dikembe and the Nuggets were one of the hottest teams in the second half of the regular season. They again clinched the final playoff spot, but this time, they were swept in the first round by the San Antonio Spurs.

The 1995 playoffs were a disappointment. But Dikembe had an outstanding season. He collected more blocked shots and rebounds than any other player. For his efforts, Dikembe was named NBA Defensive Player of the Year. It was the biggest accomplishment in Dikembe's young career. Upon winning the important award, Dikembe said "I'm very happy. It's something I've worked hard for." Dikembe pledged to work harder to make his game even better, and to help the Denver Nuggets become one of basketball's best teams.

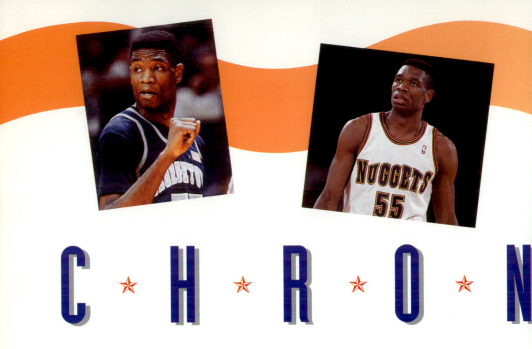

C · H · R · O · N

1966   • Dikembe Mutombo is born on June 25 in Kinshasa, Zaire.

1987   • Dikembe arrives in the United States to attend Georgetown University.

1988-89 • Dikembe leads Georgetown to the Big East Conference title.

1989-90 • In his junior season, Dikembe averages 10.7 points and 10.5 rebounds per game. He and teammate Alonzo Mourning share the Big East Defensive Player of the Year award.

1990-91 • In his senior season at Georgetown, Dikembe averages 15.2 points and 12.2 rebounds per game and is named Big East Defensive Player of the Year.
              • The Denver Nuggets select Dikembe with the fourth pick in the NBA draft on June 26, 1991.

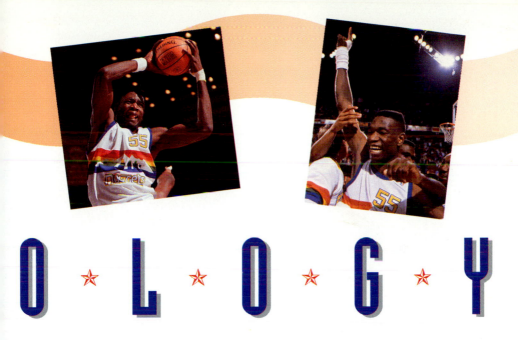

O ⋆ L ⋆ O ⋆ G ⋆ Y

1991-92 • In his standout rookie NBA season, Dikembe is the starting center for the Western Conference All-Star team.
• Dikembe is voted to the NBA All-Rookie first team.

1993-94 • In the 1994 playoffs, Dikembe leads the Nuggets to a first-round upset of the Seattle Supersonics. In the second round, Dikembe sets a playoff series record with 38 blocks against the Utah Jazz.
• In August 1994, Dikembe leads an NBA goodwill mission to Africa.

1994-95 • Dikembe is named to the Western Conference All-Star team.
• After leading the league in blocked shots and rebounds, Dikembe is named NBA Defensive Player of the Year.

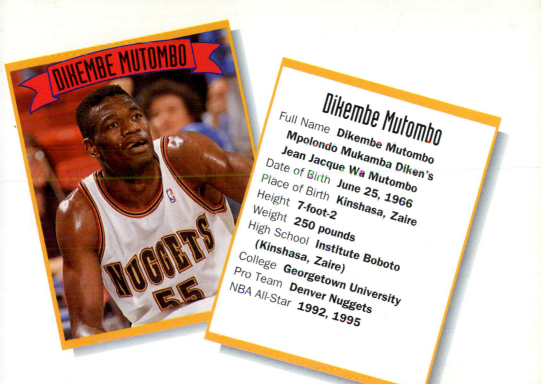

DIKEMBE MUTOMBO

Dikembe Mutombo

Full Name **Dikembe Mutombo Mpolondo Mukamba Diken's Jean Jacque Wa Mutombo**

Date of Birth **June 25, 1966**

Place of Birth **Kinshasa, Zaire**

Height **7-foot-2**

Weight **250 pounds**

High School **Institute Boboto (Kinshasa, Zaire)**

College **Georgetown University**

Pro Team **Denver Nuggets**

NBA All-Star **1992, 1995**

NBA STATISTICS

Season	Team	Scoring Average	Rebounds	Assists	Blocked Shots
1991-92	Denver	16.6	870	156	210
1992-93	Denver	13.8	1,070	147	287
1993-94	Denver	12.0	971	127	*336*
1994-95	Denver	11.5	*1,029*	113	*321*
Total (4 seasons)		**13.3**	**3,940**	**543**	**1,154**

(Numbers in *italics* indicates led league.)

★ ★ ★

About the Author

Philip Brooks grew up near Chicago and now lives in Columbus, Ohio, with his wife, Balinda Craig-Quijada. He attended the University of Iowa Writers' Workshop, where he received an M.F.A. in fiction writing. His stories have appeared in a number of literary magazines, and he has written several books for children. He is the author of *Games People Play: Japan* and *Michael Jordan: Beyond Air* (Childrens Press), and *Georgia O'Keefe* and *Mary Cassatt* (Franklin Watts).

Mr. Brooks loves to play basketball, although he blocks many fewer shots than Dikembe Mutombo.